A SPRING ART BOOK

JAPANESE NETSUKE

BY WERNER FORMAN
TEXT BY LÍDA VILÍMOVÁ
DESCRIBED BY L. BOHÁČKOVÁ
TRANSLATED BY IRIS URWIN

SPRING BOOKS · LONDON

JAPANESE

NETSUKE

Graphic design by Bedřich Forman

Designed and produced by Artia for
SPRING BOOKS
Spring House · Spring Place · London NW5
© 1960 by ARTIA
Printed in Czechoslovakia
S 853

INTRODUCTION

The traditional costume of Japan has no pockets, and the Japanese wear what the European carries in his pockets hanging from the belt at the back. The pipe-case and tobacco box (*kiseru-zutsu* and *tabako-ire*), the case for medicaments (*inro*), writing necessities (*yatate*), a bottle for *saké* rice wine (*hyotan*) and a purse for keys and money (*kinchaku*) were all hung from the belt by a cord which held them on both sides and was secured by a toggle and a slip-bead. The slip-bead was the smaller, and was slipped down over the cord to hold the articles in place; it was called the *ojime*. The toggle was larger in size and took various shapes; it was slipped up under the belt, and left hanging over. The name of the toggle, *netsuke*, comes from *ne* – a root, and *tsuke* – to fasten.

There are two main forms of *netsuke*, differing considerably from each other. Most frequently it is a flat button, either the kind known as *manju*, taking its name from a kind of round cake, and made of wood, horn, ivory and so on, ornamented in different techniques (see No. 41); the other type of *netsuke* is known as *kagamibuta* and is a round or (more rarely) square ivory button inlaid with a round plaque of a different material (usually metal) worked in relief (see No. 45).

This latter type of *netsuke* often takes on forms far removed from that of a simple toggle button. We find little carvings and figures of different materials, only a few centimetres high, representing widely different objects and often revealing their function only by the two holes bored into them. There is an infinite variety of themes, human and mythological figures, from history and from

V

everyday life, occasionally even in groups; masks used in dances in the theatre; wild animals, domestic animals and fantastic imaginary animals; tools, fruit and objects of daily life. The *netsuke* were most frequently carved from different kinds of wood, from bone and especially ivory, but metals were also used, as well as coral and semi-precious stones. There are even examples of *netsuke* made of porcelain and pottery.

Thus the *netsuke*, which was originally a necessity and an accessory to the national costume, has become a work of art which offers great possibilities to the talented craftsman, especially the sculptor and the carver. Yet we know the names of very few artists who made *netsuke* either exclusively or occasionally, and even when we know their names we know little about their lives. Their names are often known only from signatures on *netsuke* they have made, and since we do not always know whether these signatures are to be read in the Japanese or Sino-Japanese version, both forms have to be given. Few artists officially recognised and famous in other fields of art have left us *netsuke*; among them are the painter and lacquerer Ritsu-o (No. 43) and the lacquerer Korin. Carvers famous for their large masks also made small figures of the same type to serve as *netsuke*. But the vast majority of *netsuke* are by unknown craftsmen: the penetrating eye of the artist and the inimitable skill shown in the carving are all the more admirable because these *netsuke* are the work of nameless craftsmen of the people, equipped with nothing but inborn talent and a patience the European finds it hard to understand.

Another of the miracles created by this oriental virtue is lacquer work. The base of hard polished wood, iron, ivory, china or mother-of-pearl is covered by successive layers of lacquer; there may be as many as sixty layers, each oven-dried and polished. There are at least thirty processes to be gone through to produce the plain black lacquer background, before decoration with further layers of lacquer, carving, inlay work, and so on. The final work of art is not only of great artistic value, but is a miracle of durability. It is a well-known fact that Japanese lacquer work from the Vienna World Exhibition in 1873, after lying for a year and a half at the bottom of the sea in a wrecked ship, was retrieved undamaged.

The perfect technique of the Japanese master lacquerers, and the wealth of their imagination, can be seen in the *inro*, the small flat receptacle for medicaments usually divided into three or five compartments fitting closely on top of each other. As the origin of the word shows (*in* – seal, *ro* – box), the *inro* originally held seals for signing, but later they were used for medicaments, and slung from the belt on a cord held by an *ojime* and a *netsuke*.

Among the larger articles illustrated here is the *te-bako*, or toilet casket, the *ko-bako*, or incense box, and the *suzuri-bako* which held writing materials. The last-named is usually square or oblong and has a lid; it holds the ink-stone, the *mizu-ire*, or bowl for water, brushes, paper-knife and so on. In most of the plates parts of the *suzuri-bako* have been used for the background or as accessories to the main subject.

VII

DESCRIPTION OF THE PLATES

A poetess. Perhaps Murasaki Shikibu on the terrace of the Ishiyama temple, writing her famous **1**
romance *Genji-Monogatari*.
The inner side of the lid of an incense box (*ko-bako*) shaped like an oyster shell. Gold lacquer, *hira-makie* technique; 13.3 cm. wide; eighteenth century (?). Prague National Gallery.
Murasaki Shikibu was a famous beauty, a poetess who lived at the turn of the first millennium. She
was unusually talented as a child, gifted with an exceptional memory and a fine literary instinct.
She is said to have begun writing her famous chronicle of Prince Genji (a sort of Don Juan at the
Imperial Court) in the year 1001 at the instigation of the priest of the Ishiyama temple, sitting on
the temple terrace and drawing her inspiration from the moonlit Lake Biwa.
Seal signed by the painter Tan-yu and with a stylised lion. Carved ivory; 3.9 cm. wide; early nine- **2**
teenth century (?).
Kano Tan-yu or Tan-yu-sai, born 1602 in Kyoto, who also signed his work Fujiwara Morinobu,
was one of the outstanding painters of the Kano school. This school came into being in the four-
teenth century and later became the official school of painting at the court of the *shogun*. Kano
Tan-yu was particularly successful with his drawings of horses. His art, with its delicate spirituality,
was highly appreciated at court, and the *shogun* gave him the highest and most honourable titles,
hogen and *hoin*.
The lion is a frequent theme in Japanese art, but always in the typical stylised form of the chimaeric
kara-shishi, the Chinese lion which came from Buddhist India. As the king of beasts the lion guards
the holy places and is the symbol of divine protection. In Japanese art, together with the peony,
the lion is the symbol of royal power.
The background is the inside of a lacquer *suzuri-bako*, for writing materials, with a hare carved
in relief. According to legend this creature lives in the moon, grinding rice for the cakes used in
Buddhist and Shinto temple ceremonies. It lives for a thousand years, but is not one of the symbols
of longevity. It is the fourth animal in the zodiac, the symbol of the sixth hour of morning (in
Europe the fifth and sixth hours) and when used in conjunction with the cock is the symbol of the
sixth hour of the morning and the evening.

3 A toilet casket (*te-bako*) with compartments, depicting a landscape with tea-pickers. Gold lacquer (*makie* technique) on a ground of *nashiji*, aventurine lacquer, inlaid with lead and mother-of-pearl; 11.9 cm. high; eighteenth century. Prague National Gallery.

A child playing with a toy Daruma. *Netsuke*, carved ivory; 2.4 cm. high; nineteenth century. Náprstek Museum, formerly the Joe Hloucha collection.

Daruma (Sanskrit: Dharma) was the twenty-eighth Indian and first Chinese patriarch, born at the beginning of the sixth century A. D. in a royal family. He went to China and thence to Japan, passing through Korea. He was a missionary who founded the Zen sect in Japan. His name is connected with many legends, one of which led to complete profanation of the holy man's memory – he became the model for snowmen and children's weighted toys (see also No. 29). Daruma is said to have sat motionless for nine years with his legs crossed under him and his head turned to the wall in the monastery on Mount Su; his profound meditations led him to the conviction that nothing had ever existed. When he gave up his meditation at the end of nine years he found that his legs had lost their strength. Another legend adds that when a painter came to the monastery to restore the temple murals he thought the meditating saint was a weather-beaten statue and decided to restore it. When his brush touched the saint's body, Daruma was able to walk again.

A scent phial (*hioibin*). Lacquered wood (*roironuri-makie* technique), 1.8 cm. high; nineteenth century (?). Prague National Gallery.

A comb. Jade, lacquered in gold and inlaid with mother-of-pearl; 11.3 cm. long. Prague National Gallery. A comb. Jade, lacquered in gold. 10.2 cm. long. Prague National Gallery.

4 *Inro* with five compartments. Dark brown lacquer with gold relief showing a summer-house and a rolled picture, inlaid with mother-of-pearl and metal; 5.9 cm. high; early nineteenth century (?). Náprstek Museum, formerly the Joe Hloucha collection.

Kanzan and Jittoku. *Netsuke*, carved ivory; 5.9 cm. high; eighteenth century (?). Náprstek Museum, formerly the Joe Hloucha collection.

Kanzan is the Japanese name of the Taoist thinker Han-shan, who lived in China. He is often portrayed together with his friend Jittoku, to whom he is explaining the contents of a scroll he holds in his hand. Jittoku bears a broom and symbolises care for the things of this life, while Kanzan symbolises thought for higher things. These two inseparable companions spoke a language nobody understood and were therefore considered mad. But Kanzan was a talented poet whose works are still read today. Kanzan and Jittoku are also two of the 'Four Sleepers' who together with Bukan Zenshi and the tiger symbolise the complete calm of the followers of the Zen sect. They were always highly respected by the members of the sect and are sometimes thought to be the incarnation of the gods Monju and Fugen (see No. 36).

Inro with four compartments. Black lacquer decorated with wild geese in gold relief (*hiramakie* 5 technique) on a black ground (*roiro-nuri*); 6.8 cm. high; end of the eighteenth century (?). Prague National Gallery.

According to the Japanese tradition wild geese in flight carry in their beaks rushes which they drop on to the water when they are tired, and come down to rest on them. Thus they remind people of the care they should give to preparing the place where they want to settle. The geese fly in long straight rows, only breaking ranks when they see something unusual beneath them. This habit of theirs revealed to the warrior Yoshiiye and the famous archer Takenori that their enemies were hiding in the undergrowth, and thus helped them to victory.

An archer. *Netsuke*, carved ivory. 4.3 cm. high; nineteenth century (?). Náprstek Museum, formerly the Joe Hloucha collection.

This *netsuke* may depict one of the famous archers Yoyuki, Yoshiiye or Tametomo.

An unusually shaped *inro* with four compartments (see also No. 40). The wooded landscape with 6 the sun among clouds is in bas-relief on a ground of aventurine (*nashiji*) lacquer; 9.1 cm. high.

Stag lying down. *Netsuke*, carved ivory inlaid with stone; 3.7 cm. long; eighteenth century (?). Náprstek Museum.

Gama sennin. Netsuke. Carved wood; 9.4 cm. high; seventeenth century (?). Náprstek Museum, 7 formerly the Joe Hloucha collection.

The word *sennin* means a genius or a hermit, and depicts various supernatural beings both good and evil, mostly of Taoist origin. *Gama sennin*, i. e. a *sennin* with a toad, is the Taoist *sennin* Kosensei, who is said to have taken care of a very sick toad and cured it. The toad became his faithful friend and revealed itself as a demon, giving him knowledge of many secrets. According to another legend this *sennin* was a man who sold healing herbs and could change himself into a frog when he entered the water.

Background: part of a *suzuri-bako* and a pottery plate.

Inro with five compartments. A relief pattern in black and gold (*hira-* and *taka-makie* techniques) 8 of carp in the waves, with crystal inlaid on the gold background (*kinji* technique). 8 cm. high, first half of the nineteenth century. Signed Shokasai Tokujo. Náprstek Museum, formerly the Joe Hloucha collection.

A Chinese legend tells of the Dragon Gate Riyomon, through which all fish want to pass, but which can only be reached by crossing the waterfalls. Those who succeed are carried to heaven on a white cloud and live as dragons in the land of eternal happiness. Only the carp is strong and determined enough to succeed, and this makes it the personification of firm determination and perseverance. Therefore the carp is an essential part of the decorations at the boys' festival *tango no sekku* or

8 *shobu no sekku*, celebrated on the fifth day of the fifth month. Great big paper carps on bamboo poles float in the air in front of every house where there is a son, reminding him of the energy and perseverance he will need in later life.

Shokasai was a famous lacquerer of the first half of the nineteenth century who made *inro*. He usually made the faces and hands of his figures of ivory.

Background: the lid of a *suzuri-bako*.

9 A *sambaso* dancer with a rattle (*saishiki*), and the crane motif on his dress. *Netsuke*. Polychrome wood carving; 4.7 cm. high; second half of the eighteenth century (?).

The *sambaso* is an old dance formerly performed before a theatre performance was due to begin. It was originally a religious dance, and has kept its suppliant character; it was meant to placate the gods and render them indulgent to the mistakes made by the actors in the play to follow. Later the dance was meant to wish the public good luck, and was danced by men in a special costume, with a rattle and a fan in their hands. Characteristic of the costume was the high mitre-like head-dress decorated with the sun, and symbols of longevity (such as the crane) on the robe.

Background: *suzuri-bako*.

10 A boy with a *shishi* mask. *Netsuke*, pottery with partial-coloured glaze; 5.3 cm. high; eighteenth century (?).

Lion masks were used in the 'lion dance', *shishi-mai*, one of the oldest Japanese dances. Originally it was danced by one man in a big lion mask with a movable jaw; he accompanied his own dance on a little drum. Later the dance became more intricate and was danced by a group of dancers and musicians, in the form of a procession through the streets. Finally the dance became nothing more than a children's game in the New Year celebrations.

Background: a lacquer tray inlaid with egg-shells and decorated with a design of cranes in gold bas-relief.

11 An *inro* with three compartments, decorated with children's toys in relief. Deep-cut relief in gold on natural wood (*kiji-makie*); 6.2 cm. high; eighteenth century (?). Náprstek Museum, formerly the Joe Hloucha collection.

The *den-den-taiko* drum has a long handle and two movable drumsticks. The flat dolls recall the girls' festival, and the musical instruments belong to that festival too. The pipe seems to be the usual *hito-yo-kiri* five-holed flute.

The god Fukurokuju playing with a child. *Netsuke*, carved ivory; 3.5 cm. high; eighteenth century (?). Náprstek Museum, formerly the Joe Hloucha collection.

Fukurokuju is one of the seven gods of happiness. His name means 'happiness', 'wealth' and 'long life' and he is often accompanied by one of the animals symbolical of longevity – the thou-

sand-year-old tortoise, the crane or the white stag. He is considered to be the incarnation of Lao-tse **11**
himself. His most marked characteristic is the extraordinarily long head, the result of his great
wisdom and his profound meditations. This feature makes him a comic figure and robs him of all
seriousness. He is often shown as the friend of children, who play with him. In this case the child
has tied a scarf round Fukurokuju's head, either to climb up on him or to pull himself along in
the play *kubi-hiki*.

A sleeping goose. *Netsuke*, glazed pottery; 2.6 cm. high; eighteenth century (?). **12**
Background: a red lacquer tray inlaid with silver and mother-of-pearl.

New Year dancers dancing the *manzai*. *Netsuke*, carved wood; 5.5 cm. high; seventeenth century. **13**
Signed: Ichig-yoku. Náprstek Museum, formerly the Joe Hloucha collection.

The word *manzai* means the same as *banzai*, that is, ten thousand years; it is a greeting which wishes
the hearer long life. The dance of the same name is very old and was originally confined to the
Imperial court. Later it became the dance of poor wandering clowns, who performed it during the
New Year celebrations. It is also called *Mikawa-manzai*, because the people of Mikawa were particularly good at it. The chief of the dancers is called *tayu* or *manzai*, because he constantly repeats
the word while he dances, holding a fan, while the other dancer, *saizo*, accompanies him on a little
drum.

Ichig-yoku was a carver of masks in the seventeenth century.

Background: Hiroshige.

The barber's customer. *Netsuke*, carved wood; 2.9 cm. high; eighteenth century (?). Náprstek **14**
Museum, formerly the Joe Hloucha collection.

The customer, to all appearances a servant, holds in his right hand a large rolled umbrella, the
honourable symbol of his master.

Background: fragments of cloth.

An *inro* with three compartments, shaped like a bridge pile eaten away by a centipede. Black lacquer **15**
and natural wood, with deep relief in black lacquer (*kiji-makie*); second half of the eighteenth
century. Signed: Masanao. Náprstek Museum, formerly the Joe Hloucha collection.

In the tenth century there lived in Japan a famous archer, Fujiwara no Hidesato, popularly called
Tawara Toda. When Taira no Masakado revolted, Tawara Toda and Taira no Sadamori attacked
the rebel and defeated him at the battle of Kashima in 940. Tawara Toda (in other versions it was
Sadamori) cut off Masakado's head and sent it to Kyoto, for which he was rewarded with medals
and a pension. A number of legends have grown up round him, one of which inspired the artist
who made this *netsuke*. At the beginning of the tenth century the province of Omi was devastated by
a monstrous giant centipede, Mukade. No hero had succeeded in killing the monster, and they had **XIII**

15 all perished. Even the kingdom of the King of the Dragons, Ryujin, in Lake Biwa, was threatened. One day the king sent his daughter Otohime to find a hero to overcome the monster. On the bridge in Seta Otohime met Tawara Toda and told him the Dragon King's wishes. The hero went straightaway to the mountain Mikami, round which the monster lay twined seven times. He shot at it four times without hurting it in any way, and then the princess told him to lick the end of his arrow. The arrow, wet with human spittle, which is poisonous for snakes and centipedes, killed the beast. The Dragon King then richly rewarded the hero who had rid the countryside of such a terrible creature. He gave him a precious bell, a roll of brocade that had no end, a bag of rice that had no bottom, and a pot that would cook without fire. Tawara Toda later gave his precious bell to the famous temple in Miidera. The French historian Bertin gives this legend as an echo of the events round the actual rising of Taira no Masakado. Background: a nineteenth-century woodcut.

16 An *inro* with three compartments. A crane in red and gold relief, flying above the clouds (*makie*). 7.1 cm. high; eighteenth century. Signature illegible. Prague National Gallery.

The crane, in Japanese *tsuru*, is held in great honour in Japan, and together with other creatures is a symbol of longevity. In the Taoist system the crane stands for the heavenly principle, forming the foundation of the universe, while the earthly principle is represented by the tortoise. Both are characteristic inhabitants of the holy mountain, Horai (see No. 16); on the other side of this *inro* is a relief carving of the thousand-year-old tortoise on a cliff above the sea.

A tortoise on a lotus leaf. *Netsuke*, carved wood; 5.2 cm. long; nineteenth century. Signed: Tadakazu. The tortoise, in Japanese *kame*, is the second important symbol of longevity. In Taoist mythology it is one of the four supernatural animals, with the dragon, the phoenix and the tiger (or the fantastic animal, *kirin*). In Indian legend the tortoise carries on its back an elephant which holds up the world. It lives to the fantastic age of a thousand years and when it reaches this great age, it grows a strange broad tail; Japanese artists often depict it with this tail. Scientists explain this phenomenon by a plant parasite which attacks the tortoise in swamps, and forms a kind of veil at the end of its shell, reminiscent of the Japanese peasants' protection from rain, the *mino*. This thousand-year-old tortoise is therefore sometimes known as *minogame*.

17 A Chinese child (*karako*) with a little drum. *Netsuke*, ivory inlaid with mother-of-pearl, gold lacquer; 3.8 cm. high. Prague Museum of Applied Art.
Background: one of the walls of a *te-bako* (see No. 3).

18 A snail. *Netsuke*, carved wood; 3.5 cm. high; nineteenth century, signed Joshiharu.
The snail, the frog and the snake make up the trio of animals known as *san-sukumi*, the three timid ones, i. e. the three animals who are all afraid of each other. The snake can devour the frog, the frog the snail, and the snail's slime can poison the snake.

Joshiharu, who made *netsuke* in the nineteenth century, is said by writers to have come from Choshu **18**
province. On this *netsuke* the name of the place cannot be deciphered.
Background: a tray lacquered in gold on a red ground.
Three frogs. *Netsuke*, bamboo wood; 3.5 cm. long; eighteenth century (?). Prague Museum of **19**
Applied Art.
Background: *suzuri-bako*, gold lacquer inlaid with mother-of-pearl.
An *inro* with five compartments; gold lacquer with bas-relief in gold, red and silver (*hiramakie*) **20**
depicting a stone-pine by moonlight; 8.5 cm. high; eighteenth century (?). Signature illegible.
Náprstek Museum, formerly the Joe Hloucha collection.
In Japanese art the stone-pine is the symbol of strength, perseverance and happiness. Here it is
probably meant as the first, since the other side of the *inro* shows Kintoki, a legendary child of
exceptional strength, who was lost by his parents and brought up among the animals by a woman
of the woods, *yama-uba*.
An *inro* with two compartments; reddish-brown lacquer with bas-relief in gold (*hiramakie*) inlaid **21**
with mother-of-pearl; 4.5 cm. high; eighteenth century (?).
Shells. *Netsuke*, ceramics; 2.3 cm. high; eighteenth century (?).
A shell. *Ojime*, bronze; 1.5 cm. long; eighteenth century (?).
A *hi-otoko* mask. *Netsuke*, carved wood; 4.2 cm. high; nineteenth century (?). Náprstek Museum, **22**
formerly the Joe Hloucha collection.
Dancers used masks in religious ceremonies and in theatrical performances. There were many
different types; the one depicted by this *netsuke* is called *hi-otoko* or *tako* because the mouth puckered
up in the grimacing face without hair or ears makes it look like an octopus, which is called *tako*
in Japanese.
Background: the inside of a porcelain bowl.
Takara-bune, a boat with the seven gods of happiness. *Netsuke*. **23**
Carved ivory; 5.3 cm. long; nineteenth century (?).
Takara-bune is a mysterious boat which is said to sail up to the shores of Japan on New Year's
Eve, bearing treasure. Sometimes the seven gods of happiness are aboard. This group of figures,
known as *shichi-fuku-jin*, or the seven gods of home, probably came into being about the beginning
of the sixteenth century, although the individual figures comprising it were worshipped long before.
Only one of them, Ebisu, son of the first couple to create offspring, Izanagi and Izanami, is of
Shinto and therefore of Japanese origin. He is the god of trade, the protector of fishermen and
sailors, and is often shown with a large fish (*tai*). To the right of him on this picture is Daikoku,
a god of Buddhist origin, depicted usually with a hammer and a large bag for money, and accom- **XV**

23 panied by a rat, the symbol of fertility. Daikoku is the god of wealth. To the left of Ebisu is Bishamon, the Brahmin god of prosperity; he is also the god of war, when he is shown in a more terrifying form. Beyond him is the most popular of the gods of happiness, Hotei, or the hemp bag, a half Taoist and half Buddhist god. He is the god of content and moderate desires, and a great friend of children. He is often shown with a large bag, as round as the belly of the broadly-smiling god. In the middle of the back row is the only woman of the group, Benten, the goddess of pity, who is also the goddess of beauty, love, music, eloquence and the sea, and the patroness of the fine arts. She is of Brahmin origin. On her left is the god of longevity Fukurokuju (see No. 11) and in front of him Jurojin, his more serious brother, the god of longevity and wisdom; he may be another conception of the same god as Fukurokuju. In the course of time all these figures have lost their serious significance and become the familiar patrons of the Japanese home, and frequent targets for the artist's wit.

Background: *suzuri-bako*.

24 A toad. *Netsuke*, carved wood; 2.3 cm. high; second half of the eighteenth century. Signed: Masanao. According to an old legend the toad lives in the moon. It is the attribute of *Gama sennin* (see No. 7) and appears in many legends.

Masanao: see No. 15.

25 An *inro* with three compartments. Design of clouds with the god of thunder, in gold and red lacquer on plain wood (*kijimakie*) inlaid with gold wire to depict rain. 5.7 cm. high; end of the eighteenth century. Prague National Gallery.

Raiden, the god of thunder, like his companion, Futen, the god of the wind, who is often shown accompanying him (see No. 36), is usually made to look more like a demon than a god, in the Japanese mind. Legend credits him with repelling the Mongol invasion in 1281, by letting loose a furious storm and destroying the enemy fleet with his lightning.

An *ojime* in the shape of a mask of the goddess Uzume. Carved wood; 1.6 cm. high; end of the eighteenth century. Signed: Gyokuzan, Prague National Gallery.

Uzume or Okame is the Shinto goddess of mirth and sensuality. Her dancing is said to have drawn the goddess of the sun, Amaterasu, the legendary founder of the line of emperors of Japan, from the cave where she had hidden in anger, thus depriving the world of sunlight.

Gyokuzan made *netsuke* at the end of the eighteenth and the beginning of the nineteenth century. A *han-nya* mask. *Netsuke*, carved wood; 3.8 cm. high; eighteenth century (?). Náprstek Museum, Joe Hloucha collection.

The *han-nya* masks, showing a demon woman, were used in the *No* play, *Dojoji*, which is based

on an old legend about Kiyohime. She was a woman who fell passionately in love with the monk

Anchin, and when he spurned her love she tormented him in the shape of a demon snake, finally 25
killing him by casting down the monastery bell on him.

A recumbent ox. *Netsuke*, carved horn; 2.2 cm. high; eighteenth century (?). Náprstek Museum, 26
Joe Hloucha collection.

The ox, which is the symbol of spring and farming in China, in Japan is the emblem of the god of calligraphy Tenjin, a deified nobleman, Sugawara no Michizane. It is one of the signs of the zodiac, the hour of the ox being the second and third European hour, and together with the goat symbolises the eighth hour of morning and the eighth hour of evening.

A piper on an ox. *Netsuke*, carved wood; 3.5 cm. high; eighteenth century (?). Náprstek Museum, 27
Joe Hloucha collection.

A child seated on the back of an ox and playing on a flute – the picture known as *bokudo* or *ushidoji* – is a symbol of complete peace and a frequent theme in Japanese art.

Background: folk painting on paper.

Aubergine (*nasubi*) with a snail and an acorn. *Netsuke*, red, green and gold lacquer; 5.3 cm. long; 28
nineteenth century (?). Náprstek Museum, Joe Hloucha collection.

The aubergine is the symbol of favourable prophecy. To dream of Mount Fuji, two hawks and three aubergines is said to mean long life and happiness.

A wooden plate decorated in lacquer shaped with a cucumber and snail in bas-relief.

An *inro* with four compartments. Carved lacquer; 6.1 cm. high; eighteenth century (?). Náprstek 29
Museum, Joe Hloucha collection.

A melon. *Netsuke*, carved wood; 2.3 cm. high; nineteenth century (?). Náprstek Museum, Joe Hloucha collection.

Daruma. *Netsuke* made of a lacquered berry, reddish-brown lacquer. 4.1 cm. high, nineteenth century (?). Signature illegible. Náprstek Museum, Joe Hloucha collection.

Daruma: see No. 3.

A dormouse on a bunch of grapes. *Netsuke*, patinated ivory, carved and inlaid with metal; 3.5 cm. 30
high; nineteenth century (?). Náprstek Museum, Joe Hloucha collection.

Background: seventeenth-century brocade.

An *inro* with five compartments, decorated with chrysanthemums. Inlaid black lacquer (*heidatsu* 31
or *hyomon*) with gold, silver and mother-of-pearl inlay. 8.8 cm. high; nineteenth century (?).
Prague National Gallery.

The chrysanthemum, *kiku* in Japanese, is one of the most frequent motifs in Japanese decorative art. It is the emperor's flower, the emblem of Japan. It is the flower of the festival of happiness (*choyo no sekku* – the festival of chrysanthemums). Legend has it that far away there is a mountain XVII of chrysanthemums above a crystal-clear stream. Whoever drinks from this stream, into which the chrysanthemum petals fall, will live to a great old age.

A monkey with a baby monkey and pomegranates. *Netsuke*, carved ivory; 3.6 cm. high; nineteenth century. Signed: Shomin.

The monkey, *saru* in Japanese, is one of the signs of the zodiac, its hour corresponding to the sixteenth and seventeenth European hour. The combination of the monkey and the tiger represents the seventh morning and evening hours. The pomegranate is the symbol of many descendants.

It is not clear whether the name of the artist who made this *netsuke* should be read Shomin, Seimin or Masatami.

An *inro* with five compartments. Bas-relief of a chrysanthemum motif in gold on a ground of black and gold lacquer (*nashiji*); 9.4 cm. high; eighteenth century (?). Náprstek Museum, Joe Hloucha collection.

The sixteen-petalled chrysanthemum is the emblem of the emperor (see No. 31).

Background: seventeenth-century brocade and part of a *suzuri-bako*.

A monkey with a peach. *Netsuke*, carved wood; 6.3 cm. high; seventeenth century (?). Náprstek Museum, Joe Hloucha collection.

The motif of a monkey with a peach is a Taoist symbol of eternal life.

Tsuba – basket-hilt. Iron with the figure of a dragon-fly in flight in fretwork; 7.7 cm. in diameter; Sixteenth century (?). Náprstek Museum, Joe Hloucha collection.

The dragon-fly is the emblem of Japan, which used to be known as Akitsushima (*akitsu* is the old word for a dragon-fly). According to tradition the first emperor, Jimmu Tenno, went up a mountain to look over the province of Yamato, and declared that the land looked like a giant dragon-fly. The dragon-fly is also the symbol of victory and is often seen above the Imperial arms or above the chrysanthemum.

Background: a fragment of brocade.

A demon mask (perhaps the mask of the demon from the Rasho gate.). *Netsuke*, carved wood; 4.4 cm. high. Signed: Deme Sukemitsu, *tenka-ichi*.

Long, long ago the people of Kyoto were troubled by a terrible demon who lived near the Rasho gate. When the famous destroyer of demons, Minamoto no Yorimitsu, or Raiko, called upon his vassals to fight the monster, courageous Watanabe no Tsuna rose and that very night set off for the Rasho gate. All at once his horse began to tremble and a giant hand seized the hero, but he struck at it with his sword and cut it off. He put the hand in a wooden casket and told nobody. One day an old woman came to him, saying she was his old nurse; she told him stories of his childhood and asked him to show her the hand he had cut off the demon. The hero was flattered by the old woman's talk and opened the casket. At that moment the old woman turned into a witch and seized the hand. Wrapped in black clouds she disappeared.

Deme Sukemitsu was one of the three most famous members of the renowned family of carvers, Deme, who devoted themselves exclusively to the carving of masks. A literary source dated 1781 says that Deme Sukemitsu lived in Yedo and carved masks at the *shogun's* court. His work seems to have been *nagusami-bori*, that is to say, carving to pass the time. He was granted the highest title of an artist, *tenka-ichi* (see No. 16), as were two other members of the family, Deme Mitsutaka and Deme Takamitsu. The Deme family, famous carvers of masks, was descended from Jirozaemon Mitsuteru and Taikoko Koken, who were pupils of the famous monk Sankobo in the second half of the fifteenth century. There were many members of the family still carving in the eighteenth century.

A *han-nya* mask. *Netsuke*, patinated copper; 4.2 cm. high; seventeenth century. Signed: Takahisa. For *han-nya* masks, see No. 25.

Deme Takahisa was an excellent carver of masks and *netsuke* at the end of the seventeenth century. He was also called Deme Jokyu. For the story of his family, see above.

Background: brocade covering a seventeenth-century scroll.

A warrior with a shield. *Netsuke*, carved ivory – 5.1 cm. high.

Background: a wall of a *te-bako* (see No. 3).

A domestic Buddhist altar with statues of the gods Fugen and Monju; on the doors are the god of the wind, Futen, and the god of thunder, Raiden. Wood; 12 cm. high; eighteenth century (?). Náprstek Museum, Joe Hloucha collection.

Fugen Bosatsu (Samantabhadra) is a Buddhist god, Buddha's favourite pupil. He is usually seated on the elephant 'of the good law' and is the personification of piety and prayer. Monju Bosatsu (Manjusri) is the highest god of supernatural wisdom and is usually portrayed seated on a lion. Futen and Raiden: see No. 25.

The goddess Okame. *Netsuke*, ceramics; 3.2 cm. high; eighteenth century (?). Náprstek Museum, Joe Hloucha collection.

Okame, or Uzume: see No. 25.

An *inro* with five compartments. Carved in red lacquer (*tsuishu*) with bamboo in gold bas-relief on a silver-grey ground (*shibuichiji*); 9.5 cm. high; early nineteenth century. Signed: Kansai-sha, i. e. drawn by Kansai or copied after Kansai.

Bamboo, *take* in Japanese, is the most important Japanese plant. The Japanese use it to build their homes, to make many things of daily life, as material for works of art, and the young shoots as food. The bamboo is the symbol of long life, steadfastness and fidelity. The tiger hiding behind

37 the bamboo from the storm, (*take ni tora*), symbolises the helplessness of earthly power before the force of the elements.

Koma Kansai (died 1835) was one of the last famous artists of the Koma family. He worked in Yedo at the end of the eighteenth and the beginning of the nineteenth century. He was famed for his fine carvings in the *chinkibori* technique. All the members of the Koma family were famous lacquerers, and worked at the court from 1663 to 1835.

A tigress with her young. *Netsuke*, carved ivory with eyes of inlaid semi-precious stones; 3.8 cm. high; nineteenth century (?). Náprstek Museum.

Like the lion, the tiger is a stranger to the Japanese islands, and was usually portrayed in the traditional manner taken over from China. It is assumed to be a mythical beast and is the symbol of courage. Painted on the doors of offices it is meant to rouse in the visitor the feelings of fear and awe. It is said to live a thousand years. When it reaches the age of five hundred a character meaning 'king' is said to appear on its head, and at the age of a thousand it becomes an inhabitant of the Milky Way.

38 Chokaro. *Netsuke*, carved wood; 4.2 cm. high; nineteenth century. Signed: Yumehachi.

Chokaro or Tsugen is one of the eight immortal genii of Taoism. He is said to have lived in the seventh and eighth centuries, and to have been remarkable for his magic strength and his learning. The emperor himself offered him the hand of his daughter and high office, but Chokaro refused, preferring freedom and the company of his strange white horse. This horse could carry him to the most distant places in a few moments; he needed no fodder, and when the wise man did not need him, he could be tucked away in a gourd, whence he readily jumped out when his master had need of him and licked the mouth of the gourd.

It is not clear whether this figure was used as a *netsuke*, for it does not possess the traditional two holes for the cord, usually found even where the configuration of the *netsuke* makes them unnecessary. It is probably a false *netsuke* (*okimono*, or article to be stood up). In favour of this theory, is the fact that the blade of a miniature sword can be drawn out of the scabbard by Chokaro's side. The *netsuke* is standing on the edge of a glazed ceramic bowl.

39 An *inro* with five compartments (see No. 31).

The butterfly (in Japanese *cho*) was thought to be the incarnation of the soul of a living person. It is a good sign if a butterfly flutters into the house, but sometimes the butterfly is a foreteller of death or the incarnation of a soul getting ready to leave its body. A lonely old man is said to have begged his niece to come and live with him in case he needed help. He did indeed soon fall ill, and the niece together with her son looked after the old man. One day the boy was sitting by the old man's bed when he saw a big white butterfly on the pillow. After a while it fluttered off to the graveyard and

settled on a tombstone, before disappearing. The boy ran to see the name on the tombstone where
the butterfly settled. It was the grave of a girl called Akiko, who had died young; although old,
the grave was covered with fresh flowers. When the boy got back the old man was dead. The boy
told his mother about the butterfly and she remembered that Akiko had been the old man's betrothed, and had died just before the wedding. The young man had then sworn never to marry,
but to stay near her. The butterfly was the man's soul incarnate following his betrothed.

A tortoise. *Netsuke*, carved black stone; 4.6 cm. long; nineteenth century (?). Náprstek Museum.

Inro (see No. 6).

A mouse. *Netsuke*, wood; 2 cm. high; nineteenth century. Signed: Masabumi. Náprstek Museum,
Joe Hloucha collection.

The mouse or rat (in Japanese *nezumi*) is one of the signs of the zodiac, its hour lasting from eleven
at night until one in the morning after the European fashion. It is also linked with Daikoku, the
god of wealth. There is a legend that the Buddhist idols observed that the practical Japanese were
sacrificing to Daikoku, from whom they hoped to get wealth, and neglecting them. They asked the
god of the underworld, Emmu, to put things right. He sent a powerful demon to earth to get rid
of their divine competitor. Led by a sparrow, the demon went to Daikoku's home, but found him
out. At last he found him sitting comfortably on the bales of rice in a great merchant's house.
He hid so as to take Daikoku by surprise, but his intended victim had heard footsteps and sent
his chief rat to see who had come in. The rat discovered the demon and ran into the garden for
a twig of holly and drove the terrified demon back to the gates of hell with it.

A mouse on a pod. *Netsuke*, carved wood; 2.3 cm. high, eighteenth century (?). Náprstek Museum,
Joe Hloucha collection.

An *inro* with five compartments. Bas-relief of the holy mountain of immortality. Horai, on gold
lacquer (*kinjimakie*) with metal inlaid; 8.2 cm. high; eighteenth to nineteenth centuries.
Signed: Kajikawa, the mark of the Kajikawa family. Náprstek Museum, formerly the Joe Hloucha
collection.

The mythical mountain Horai is one of the three islands of paradise inhabited by genii who drink
from the spring of immortality. Pine trees, plum trees, peach trees and holy fungus grow here,
and the thousand-year-old tortoise and the cranes live here. The island stands on the shell of a giant
tortoise.

Kajikawa Kyujiro was one of the most famous lacquerers of the seventeenth century. He worked
at the *shogun's* court in Yedo, and died in 1682. He enjoyed the title of *tenka-ichi*, the first
below heaven, which was the highest honour, given only to exceptional artists. His descendants
were also called Kyujiro and signed their work Kajikawa; they were all great artists. The family

41   was still active in the nineteenth century, but it was in the eighteenth century that their finest work was produced.

A *netsuke* of the *manju* type, depicting a crane. Carved ivory and metal; 4.5 cm. across; eighteenth century. Prague National Gallery.

42   A mermaid. *Netsuke*, carved wood; 3.8 cm. long; nineteenth century. Signed: Mairyo (?).

Ningyo, literally man-fish, are the mythical inhabitants of the land of Tai-yan. Their heads and shoulders are human but their bodies those of a fish. They listen to the murmur of the shells and learn from them the secrets of the depths of the sea. In Japanese art they are almost exclusively represented as women.

The carver of this *netsuke* has signed himself with the characters *mai, tsune* – every man, and *ryo, yoi* – good. It is not clear whether the name should be read in the Japanese way as Tsuneyoshi or Tsunenaga, or in Sino-Japanese as Mairyo.

Background: the inside of the lid of a *suzuri-bako*.

43   An *inro* with three compartments. Rough lacquer on wood with a coloured ceramic relief of a stag, a golden yellow bas-relief of the moon and maple leaves; 7.2 cm. high; seventeenth to eighteenth century. Signed: Shoko, with the seal of Kan. Náprstek Museum, Joe Hloucha collection.

The Japanese deer, *shika*, is smaller and more slender than the European deer, and spotted like a fawn. Holy deer are kept at the shrine of Kasuga in Nara; they are dedicated to one of the three gods worshipped in the temple there. The deer is the symbol of autumn, especially when it appears in conjunction with the red leaves of the maple. It is often depicted with Jurojin (see No. 23) for it is another symbol of longevity.

Ogawa Ritsu-o (1663—1747) who also signed his work Shoko and added a faience seal of the character Kan, was one of the greatest of all Japanese artists. His real name was Haritsu, and he was born in the province of Ise. He was a contemporary and pupil of the greatest master of lacquering, Ogata Korin, and a pupil of Korin's brother Kanzan for the art of ceramics. He was also an outstanding Tosa painter and a poet. In his lacquer work he drew inspiration from the work of Honami Koyetsu (1556—1637), Korin's famous precursor, a painter and lacquerer, and for his encrustation work he used not only lead, mother-of-pearl and pewter, but coral, horn and especially faience and porcelain. He liked to imitate old coins, old mirrors, green with patina and so on. He applied his decorations to lacquered wood, but most of all to plain wood. He founded a school, and one of his pupils was Hanzan.

A group of mushrooms. *Netsuke*, carved wood; 3.6 cm. high; second half of the eighteenth century. Signed: Masanao. Náprstek Museum. Masanao: see No. 15.

Background: part of a *suzuri-bako*.

An *inro* with four compartments. Large gold flakes (*okibirame*) on a ground of aventurine lacquer
(*nashiji*), and sparrows in various shades of gold leaf; 6.8 cm. high; c. 1700 (?). Prague National
Gallery. The sparrow (in Japanese *suzume*) is often depicted in conjunction with the bamboo; *fukura-suzume*, a puffed-up sparrow, is the frequently used stylised form. A folk tradition has it that the soul
of Fujiwara Sanekata, who died of exhaustion and hunger in exile on the island of Oshu, was changed
into a flock of sparrows who flew to the Emperor's courtyard and fed on the rice scattered for them
there. These sparrows are called *nyu-nai-suzume*, sparrows who go into the palace. There is a folk
tale of a man who wanted to give his overlord a special present, and sent to China for a number
of sparrows. One of them dying on the way, the original fellow added a Japanese sparrow to make
up the number. The overlord was impressed by this magnificent gift, but wondered why there
was one Japanese sparrow among the Chinese birds. His vassal answered: 'They are all foreigners,
so I thought they had better have an interpreter.'

A sparrow (*fukurasuzume*). *Netsuke*, carved wood: 5.2 cm; c. 1700 (?). Signed: Goro (?). Náprstek
Museum, Joe Hloucha collection.

An *inro* with three compartments decorated with hunting emblems. Reddish-brown lacquer inlaid
with ivory, mother-of-pearl and metal; 7.1 cm. high; eighteenth century (?). Náprstek Museum,
Joe Hloucha collection.

A *netsuke* of the *kagamibuta* type representing an archer. Beaten metal inlaid with gold on a foundation of ivory; 4.5 cm. across; nineteenth century (?). Náprstek Museum, Joe Hloucha collection.

An *inro* with four compartments. Black lacquer with high gold relief inlaid with mother-of-pearl
in a design of stylised leaves of the *icho* tree; 11.2 cm. high.

The *icho* (*gingko biloba*, *Salisburia adiantifolia*) is a needle-bearing tree which reaches a height
of eighty-two feet and has its needles arranged fanwise. It often appears as a decorative motif
in Japanese art. There is an old superstition that the cones of this tree have magic power to protect
whoever carries them against attack by foxes. In popular Japanese thought the fox, like the badger,
is an animal endowed with demonic powers and determined to do all possible harm to man. Another
useful quality of the *icho* tree is that of revealing the slightest amount of poison present in food
or drink, by a quiet crackling sound.

A dragon. *Netsuke*, carved ivory; 5.3 cm. broad; eighteenth century (?).

Of all the supernatural beasts the dragon is the most frequent in oriental art. Japanese folk tradition
and art took the dragon over from China along with its symbolic significance and a whole series
of legends. As in China the dragon is the emperor's symbol, but only the five-clawed dragon.
According to legend the first emperor, Jimmu Tenno, was the son of the daughter of the Dragon
King, Princess Toyotamahime. The dragon has a number of remarkable attributes: for instance,

46 it can change its size at will from one extreme to the other, and can become invisible. Its breath becomes a cloud from which water or fire rains. It has altogether more to do with water than with fire, and often appears in the clouds. Even this powerful creature, however, has its enemies, and one of these is the centipede. It is frightened of five-coloured silk and does not like iron. It is devoted to Buddha and his followers, and is often shown in their company. The dragon is also a sign of the zodiac, its hour being between the seventh and ninth morning hour, corresponding to the eighth and ninth hour of the European day. Together with the dog the dragon is the sign of the fifth morning and evening hours of the Japanese day.

The Japanese maple (*momiji*) is famous for the wonderful beauty of its leaves, which change colour particularly in the autumn. To send a packet of maple leaves to someone means to jilt one's lover. This allegory contains a Japanese pun: 'As the colour (*iro*) of these leaves changes, so does my love (*iro*).'

47 An *inro* with two compartments. A design of maple leaves in red and gold lacquer on plain wood (*kijimakie*); 5 cm. high; seventeenth century (?). Prague National Gallery.

The symbolical significance of the maple as a sign of autumn is stressed by two deer on the other side of the *inro*.

A toad. *Netsuke*, pottery glazed white; 4.8 cm. long; eighteenth century (?).

48 Hotei with a child and a scroll. *Netsuke*, carved ivory; 3.6 cm. high; early nineteenth century. Signed: Masatoshi.

Hotei: see No. 23.

Masatoshi was an excellent carver of *netsuke* at the end of the eighteenth and beginning of the nineteenth century.

Background: a scarf with characters printed on it, used by students to wrap up their school things.

49 Two fishes. *Netsuke*, carved wood; 3 cm. high; eighteenth century. Signed: Sukesato. Náprstek Museum.

Ground and background: a *suzuri-bako*.

50 A Chinese lady with a basket. *Netsuke*, carved wood; 7.5 cm. high; eighteenth to nineteenth century. Signed: Namboku.

Background: a *suzuri-bako*.

PLATES

My hands were too weak to hold you back when you had made up your mind to leave me. Time gave the command. You disappeared as suddenly as a tiny cloud on the horizon. Like the Northern Star with its dazzling cold gleam, fading from sight in the light of dawn. It is hard to believe you are no longer here. My loneliness rocks my forsaken heart like a mother lulling her sick child. I seek you everywhere. My fingers move over the walls, with the palm of my hand I timidly caress your place. Your sandals of straw, your pipe grown cold, your porcelain cups. Your inro inlaid with mother-of-pearl and your tiny netsuke – is that all that is left of these days we have lived through? Yet you talked of eternity. How short it was, your eternity! I am going to write to you. I shall write in the bright morning sun when the scent of the flowers just unfurling their petals comes tiptoeing in to greet me. In the quiet of twilight when endless shrouds of mist awaken autumn sadness. In the long nights when terror breaks into peaceful slumbers. My memories as painful as an open wound, my infinite longing as broad as the ocean, my fear and my hopes, my thoughts and the modest joys of everyday life – all this I will put into black characters, taking ink and brush. The whole of my life will be printed on these pages like a changing picture. You will never read them. Just as you will never know of my sorrow. I shall let them float away on the water. The dancing patches of light, like the splinters of a mirror, will break up what I have written and the characters will bob up and down on the water. They will swirl round in the whirlpool and disappear into the rushes. Not even the shadow of them will remain...

I

My seal has locked the letter with a thousand keys. It is heavy, heavy indeed. How can paper bear such a weight of longing and sadness? How shall I send it? Who will deliver it to you? The messenger's bag is too small, no horse could carry it, no bird's wings bear it aloft. It is like a mountain of stone, like Fudji Mountain. Perhaps you will laugh as you break the seal. How stupid she is, how silly, you will say to yourself. Why is she so sad, what is she sorrowing for, when the sun is shining and the warm breeze tells us spring is on the way? You had better not read it. Do not even open it. I know you have forgotten by now, and never even think of me. What could my words have to tell you? Do not read them. But when you go to sleep at night, lay my letter on your chest. Then you will feel how heavy is the heart that loves...

My comb fell today, when I was doing my hair in the morning. For whom do I coil my hair, for whom do I paint my face and rub scented ointments on my neck and arms? I am alone, all alone. If you were to come... If a great miracle were to happen and you were to appear suddenly in my doorway... You would let down my hair, my long hair as black as ebony, which has taken me so long to arrange. You would let my hair slip through your slim fingers like a stream of water, running over your palms; you would plunge right into it like the waves of the sea, and then you would gently unbutton my robe... And then the silly trifles – combs, flasks, my lacquer box – would stop laughing at me for wasting my time with them.

They are like the sparrows. Free and bound by no home, lingering where they will, this morning they suddenly appeared before my gate. First they looked round timidly, as if they were afraid of some fierce dog, and then one of them lightly took a roll of parchment from his sleeve, and they began to sing. Like a bubbling spring their song leaped over the fence as light as a dragonfly. It rose in a fountain like the fireworks on festival days, and lingered on the wind like the last leaf torn from the bough… At least there are people who can give pleasure with their song.

4

Above my head the wild geese are flying south. Autumn leaves as red as drops of blood are tossing in the wind. By morning a tiny spider had hung upon the bushes his silver thread. The golden brown chrysanthemum blooms are waiting humbly, as I am, for the first rays of the weak sun to touch them. Today they fall slowly, slipping gently over the damp sandy roads. Not a frog is left croaking by the pond, hidden beneath a lotus leaf. The beetles have crawled deep down into the ground and the rainbow hues of the butterflies no longer flutter in drunken dance above the grass. It is quiet everywhere, quiet. Only high up, far above my head, the wild geese are flying like a snow-white cloud... Down there on the slope an unknown marksman appears from nowhere, like an evil dream, and turns his bow against the sky. He stands motionless, his chest thrust out and head thrown back, as if he had turned to stone. Everything is trembling, the bushes and the greying grass, the high branches of the pine trees, the transparent veils of gossamer. I too am trembling... He has loosed his arrow. And silence has fallen again. The cloud passes on and drops of blood are tossing in the wind.

The moon is a porcelain plate hanging among the clouds. The trees have turned to snow-white lace. If the ground were not as hard as rock, if the wild creatures were not wandering starving through the woods — how lovely it would be to dream of early spring mornings.

Snow has fallen and hunger creeps through the land as dead as the moon. Frozen branches point towards the sky like phantoms and lean stray dogs leave deep tracks behind them on the ground. A wandering monk is going from village to village, preaching death and destruction to all he meets. He looks into your eyes with grim rejoicing, and fills you with dread. Where has he come from and what does he want? He comes uninvited and knocks at the door with his bony hand. You cannot keep him out by shutting the door. A phantom of midnight. Death.

I shall be grateful to you as long as I live for that short time we spent together. For the ecstasy with which you flooded my heart, may lasting happiness accompany you on life's road. Although a fateful moment transformed reality so soon into a fleeting vision, I look at the morning with other eyes, bowing low to the beauty hidden in the dew on the humble grass. For all this wealth — how poor is my wish for you, coming in this letter instead of a New Year's gift.

Bells were jingling in the streets until morning came, and the white snow was falling all night. The soft white flakes came floating down to earth like herons' feathers. Drums were throbbing and trumpets blaring, and the lighted lanterns were like fallen stars wandering through the town. Towards midnight I went out on to the terrace; the snowstorm had piled a high drift before my door. I looked into the eyes of a merry clown, drunk with wine and intoxicated by the pleasant company of his fellows. He laughed and laughed, swaying from the waist, and sweat poured down his flushed cheeks. Then he stumbled on, wavering through the darkness and the dancing snowflakes.

A determined child is standing and gazing into the distance. What do his eyes see, I wonder? Mysterious beings fluttering through a child's dreams like birds' wings? I wonder what we elders have done that the gates of the kingdom of fantasy are closed to us for ever?

Youth when it has fled is like a broken toy. Before we have even begun to know its fragile charm, all that is left is a bit of splintered wood and coloured paper. We play with our toys too carelessly, like a child whose hands are too eager.

I must tell you this. A tremendous change came overnight, as if a magician had waved his wand. The cherry tree in the middle of the garden covered itself in blossom by the morning. I stood and looked at it in silence, afraid the vision might fade away. The air was so fresh, there were great drops of dew trembling in the grass, and a white duck came swimming down the stream. I do not know what it is like where you are, but here spring has come...

Wandering clowns came to bring mirth to the sad. They pull funny faces and dance and sing, beating time on their little drums. Everyone has the right to buy amusement. But who will comfort the two wanderers as they go away from the town, hungry and weary? They have hearts like the rest of us – glad to give freely of mirth, but full of pain and tears.

The streets are full of noise and many colours. Full of clowns and full of people. The dyers are dyeing cloth, the cooks cooking bowls of white rice, the barbers are shaving hair grown long, the shopkeepers are measuring silk by the yard. There are fish for sale, and bamboo shoots, baskets of fruit, sticks of incense; the wandering monk would even sell you a slice of Heaven. Come and buy, come and buy, they are all shouting and pulling you by the sleeve. But where happiness can be bought, none of them can say.

Love is a firm bridge joining two banks. You and me. The bridge piles stand firm and never shift even when the muddy torrent comes swirling round them. But within, woodworm is eating away the heart of the wood to bring the bridge down like a child's toy. Woodworm – the evil tongues that wish us no good.

Like two trees with branches intertwined – we shall live together forever. What if the wind tear us apart after a while, bending one this way, one that. It will right us again, and in the spring we shall be covered in blossom. And when our strength fails and our grey heads are too heavy, we will wait for the cranes to pass over the sky. Freed of our earthly bonds we shall rise with them, soaring above the earth.

*Summer is running throughout the land and beating his little drum. Bim – bam – bom…
you can hear it everywhere. It is beating in the meadows and on the hillside, the clear metallic
tone rings far and wide. The village women are gathering their juicy fruit in baskets, in the
fields they are binding sheaves of rice, and the air is full of scents and the humming of bees.
Just like that day… do you remember? We sat down under an old willow tree and the leafy
branches hid us from the eyes of the world like a green curtain. We lay on the ground and
gazed up at the mysterious characters written against the sky by the willow leaves, as if
someone had written a long poem there with his brush. The water lapped at our feet and
now and again a silver-bellied fish leapt above the ripples; your breath scorched my cheek.
Suddenly we heard a strange sound near by and fled in confusion through the tall grass.
Who was it that frightened us so, who had found out our secret hiding-place? Silly – it was
only summer passing by and beating out the alarm on his little drum.*

I am watering the irises. The drops of water trickle down the leaves and the earth greedily drinks up the silvery streams. Tiny pearls gleam in the flowers; the sun has breathed a rainbow into each. Like a snail lazily laying his sticky track, so is the day drawn out for me, so slow, my love...

A green bamboo stalk has come through the earth's crust. Every day it grows taller and taller, striving higher and higher. It must nearly be touching the birds as they fly, the blue vault of heaven, the sun and the constellations. Can pride be left to reach the very skies? One morning men will come from the village and bury their axes deep in the pith. The slender bamboo trunk will fall to the ground and lie there, dead and helpless. How fortunate the painter came secretly with brush and ink, to portray its likeness and its form for eternity!

The crescent moon floats like a boat over the black stream of night. Far below her a silver pathway lies across the water. The moonbeams falling. Like gleaming fish scales, like tiny scraps of gilt, they tremble, reflect the light, glitter – who has scattered them on the water? I lean over from the bank and dip my hand into the water. I will catch a few of these tiny gold coins. I could remain, lifting them out until morning. They would only glitter for a moment in the palm of my hand, and then fall back into the depths again.

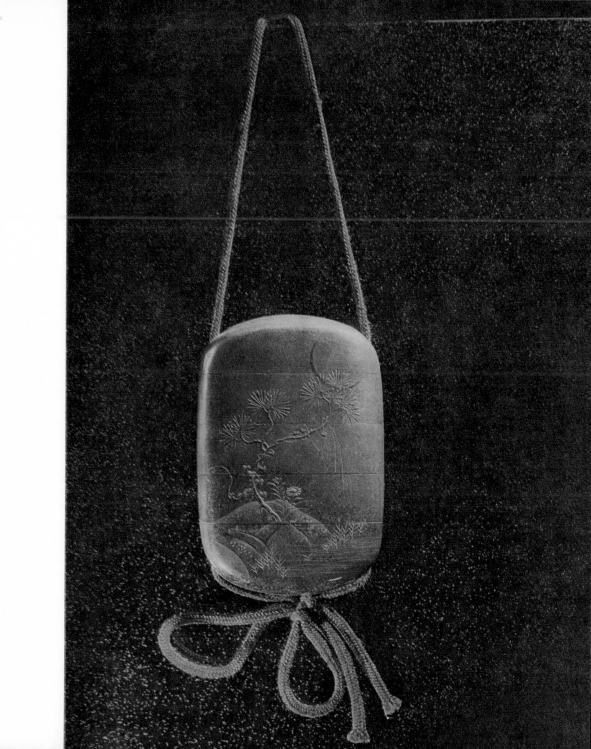

I walk by the seashore and gather cockle shells and mother-of-pearl. The surf soothes the seagulls' cries. Did you say: think of me? Or was it: don't forget? I gaze into the water, seeking your reflection by the side of mine. The image ripples and breaks in wider and wider circles, the sea carries it away...

The seaweed floating in the clear water is like a network of fine veins, or like the swaying of long hair in the wind. Why do the octopus heads lie in wait on the sandy floor like murderers, on the look-out for foolish fishes? I thought there was a happier world down there under the water than the one we live in above.

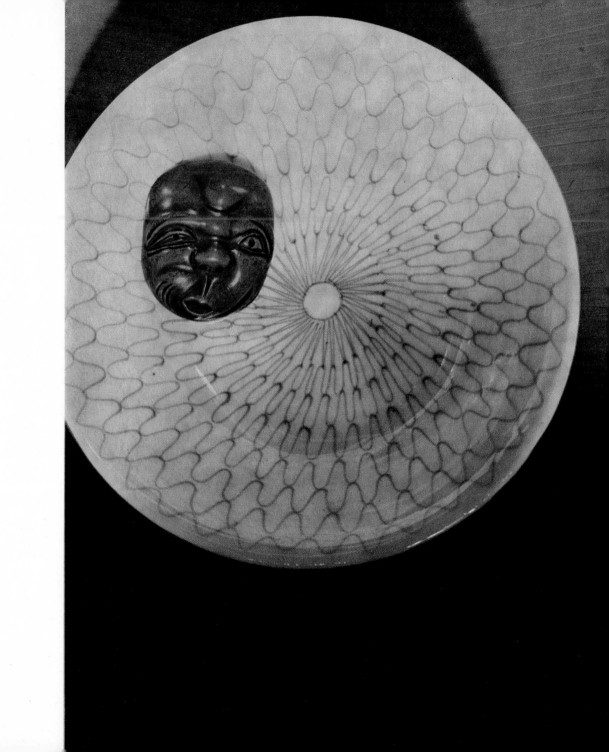

A merry company is gliding down the stream, the water lapping softly at the oars. The night is warm and as intoxicating as wine; even the moon has set out on her wanderings with her twin. One of them is up in the sky and the other near at hand, gliding over the dark water like a shadow. The fisherman's line flies through the air like an arrow. But take care – the boat is not very steady, there is wine to drink – and you cannot fish the moon out.

Even if I went to lie down on my mat, I could not sleep. What a noise the frogs in the pond are making tonight. Is it a funeral song, or is some little frog with a garland on her head celebrating her betrothal? The night passes like a barefooted pilgrim leaning on a stick, and the proud army of the stars follows it. When their glitter dies away the east will be flooded with an opal mist. The last frog among the lotuses is still sending his monotonous song to the heavens. Even the cold heart of a frog needed to sob out such excessive longing...

Sometimes joy comes after sorrow. Smiles appear through the curtain of tears. After a night marked by storms with the seal of evil, the new day awakens like a child with clear, happy gaze. But what is that to me, when the loveliest blooms in my garden are lying broken on the ground?

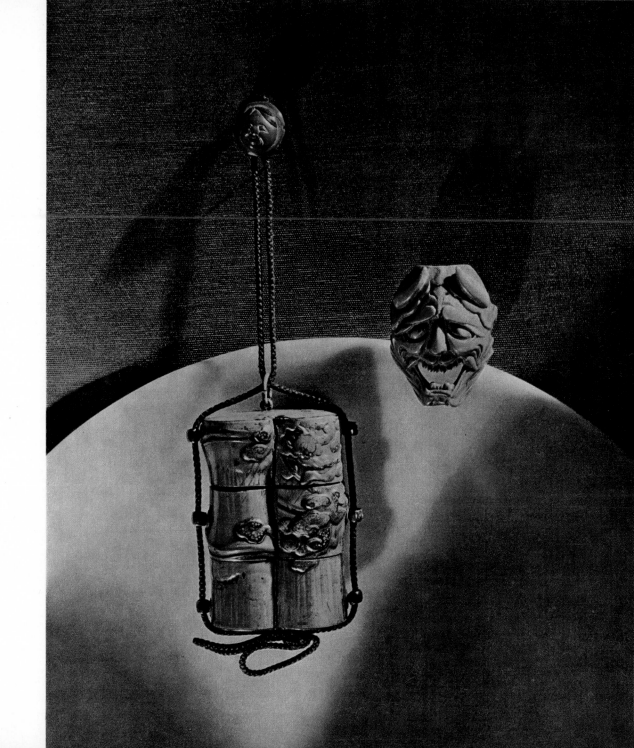

The sunset clouds have cast a glow of mother-of-pearl over the tops of the pine trees, and it glides down into the valley. The water-buffaloes, tired with the day's ploughing, sink heavily to rest in the rough grass; motionless, they look like figures carved in stone. Overgrown summer-houses crouched on the hillsides seem to be in flames. Down the evening breeze comes the sad note of a shepherd's flute. Like a white phantom my Mount Fudji gleams in the distance...

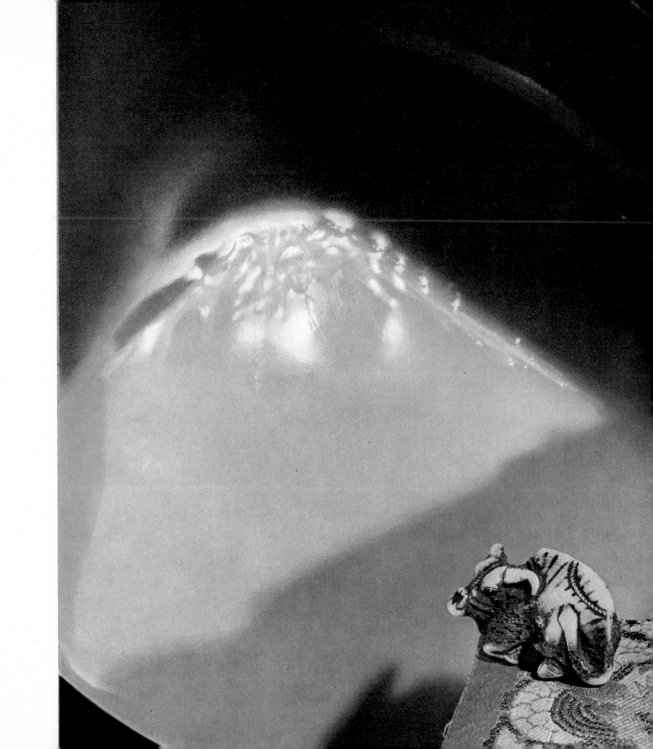

A villager riding on the back of a water-buffalo is moving slowly away on the road up to the mountains, like a boat, moving over meadows and darkening hillsides. He sinks slowly into the smoke of evening fires, and as he goes he sings of the long August nights. His song trails behind him like a ball of silk. He is further and further away – now he is only a vague outline, a grey shadow in eternity…

I wish I could take a pilgrim's staff and set out to look for you at the end of the world. How can I let you know that the beans behind the house are ripening? I gather them into my basket – and each one reminds me what it was like in spring, when the red beanflowers bloomed.

And the pumpkins. How proudly they swell in their little plot, among the twisting weeds! Why are they so proud that a drunken summer noon has transformed their delicate blossoms into these shapeless heavy bodies on the ground? The ripe fruit makes orange patches which straggle sensually over the emerald-green palette.

The sweet juice is pressed from the clustering grapes. The greedy insects gather to suck — even a little dormouse has been lapping at it until he is quite drunk. The wine confuses my mind until I find myself drinking by moonlight to one who is far away.

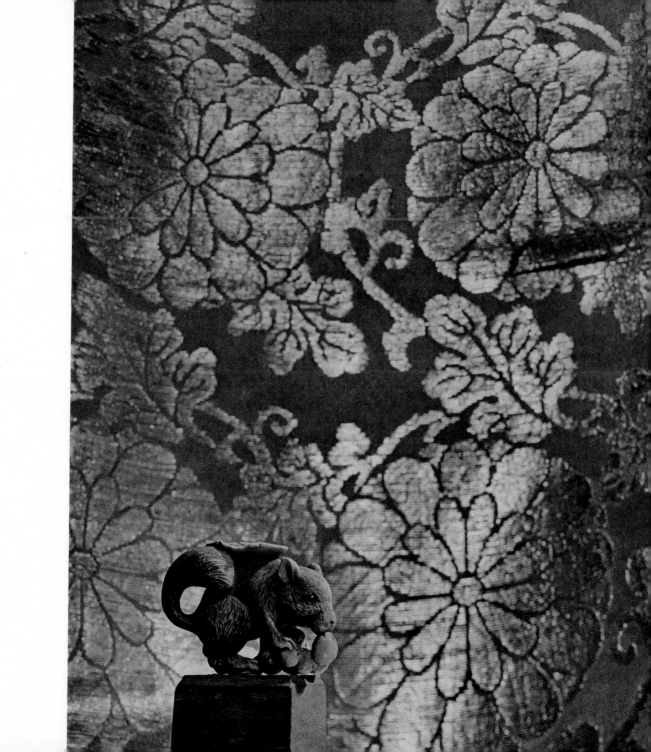

I am like a tall blade of grass forgotten and out of place in a bunch of flowers. A fan of all colours glows around me, but I bow in shame to the ground as if I were clad in nun's garments. How can a dusty blade of grass hope the butterfly will rest his azure wings on her even for a moment?

I send you three chrysanthemum petals in my letter today – three humble serving-maids to bow at your feet. One will take off your sandals, another will smooth the folds of your kimono and the third will hand you a bowl of clear golden tea. They will be shy, perhaps, and clumsy – for they have never been alone with a man before. Three little serving-maids – three petals of chrysanthemum.

A dream — a transparent dragonfly with bluish wings, hovering here and there in its dance through the air. It is gone before you can stretch out your hand. Often I dream that we are walking through an unknown country together, hurrying to arrive as soon as we can — where? How can I tell, when I always waken as day breaks?

Feverish chimaeras haunt my dreams. Unspoken terror dogs my steps like a shadow. As I put a twig of flowering wistaria into a porcelain vase, I feel a poisonous breath over my shoulder. Not for a moment do I forget that all the delicate beauty conjured up can be destroyed in a flash by the devil's anger.

All night long the dogs were howling as though there was somebody hidden at the back of the house. Then people brought strange rumours from the market-place, making my retreat uneasy. Their tongues flash like flames, they cut like sharp knives, they crush like thunderbolts. My smile must not betray what is aching within my breast. What strange people! They will be here again tomorrow, I am sure, quite sure. But tonight I shall silence the dogs, whoever may be wandering round my house. What does it matter to us, if we have each other – you me, and I you.

Fires are raging in a far-off land. Horses are rearing in battle. Who will protect you from the arrows of the foe? My bent head, my everlasting embroidering? May the gods hear my ardent prayers. May they accept the offering I burn at the altar in your name every day.

If you should fall in battle... If your horse should paw the ground helplessly... I would come to bind up your wounds. With my white scarf I would wipe the sweat from your brow. Day and night I would watch by your bedside, as quietly as the foam on the river, crouching humbly at your door. I would watch over your every breath, I would mend the rents in your cloak. I would kiss every tiny tear through which the red drops of your blood poured.

37

A flat gold disk is mirrored in the night sky like the eye of a dead fish. Midnight is long past. The wind rushes wildly through the night, dragging tattered clouds across the moon's face. It beats wildly at the boughs of the trees and tears at the sails of the fishermen's boats at sea. Wilder still is the haste of the mysterious rider. His horse's hoofs thunder on the rock, scattering stones as they strike. Where has this rider come from, what is he doing here, why does he spur his horse so over unknown paths? Has he been sent here? Is someone waiting for him? Now, in the middle of the night? Is the news he brings good or bad? The thunder of hoofs draws nearer, now he has jumped the ditch, now he is climbing higher and higher up the hillside. I am trembling with apprehension: should I pour a goblet of wine for the rider and draw water from the well for his steed? or should I veil my face in mourning?

Today I pulled the first white hair from my head. I have twisted it round my finger. Perhaps you will ask me who gave me a silver ring. And I shall answer: the most faithful of friends – time.

I could not get to sleep last night. I felt there was somebody walking about the house. Light steps sounded everywhere. I took a lantern and went to see. Who do you think had come to pay me a visit? Little grey mice with eyes like beads; they scuttled away into their holes in fright. They had come to see what my brush had been painting so long on the yellow rolls today.

We found each other too late in this world. A butterfly will sometimes settle on the plum blossom when it is dropping. The pollen has been blown away by the wind and insects have sucked all the sweet honey. But after we are dead, in some other world, perhaps we shall belong to each other as night to day. Even the plum will blossom again when the crane flies over to herald another spring.

My jade pin fell into the sea. It was a present from you. You didn't mean anything when you fixed it in my hair. And I, poor fool, thought it was a symbol of your eternal friendship. Perhaps the waves will carry it away; perhaps some tiny water fairy far below the sea will take my pin eagerly, to put in her transparent robe.

Today I picked up the first leaf that fell silently on to the path. Do you know what that means? It is the end of summer, the end of the long days and clear nights, the end of everything that danced so madly under the blue sky. Like when a path suddenly ends deep in the woods, like when a pilgrim stops short in amazement at the edge of a precipice. What will come next? Tell me, tell me what I shall have to comfort me when the birds grow silent and the last leaves fall to the ground from the trees?

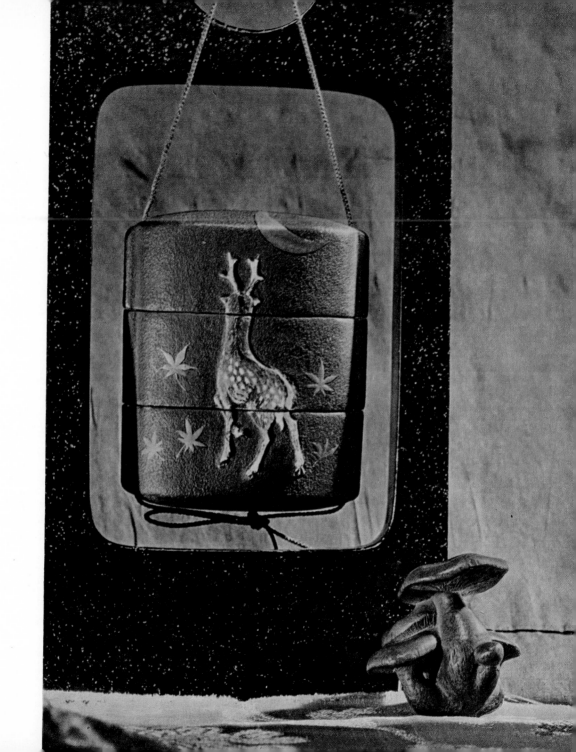

My thoughts are like a flock of sparrows. Startled by people's voices, they fly away on all sides. Uneasily they hide in the branches of the trees. In a little while they will fly down again, twittering and fluffing out their feathers, flying into one another and swooping up and down. As twilight begins to fall they loyally fly together and set off all in the same direction. The dust rises a little as they go, and a grey feather twists gently down through the air.

Dogs were barking in the woods, and arrows flew into the tree trunks. Who would not wish the hunters luck as they spur their horses up the hillside after their prey? But how could I refuse shelter to the shy doe fleeing before them and seeking refuge in my home?

When you went away the morning was cool and the leaves on the trees were fresh and green. Now autumn-tinted leaves are falling on to my hair from those same trees. Kites on their strings are climbing into the air and still you do not come. Nothing is changed...

A frog is dozing in the avenue, so still. The ground is covered with gold and copper. The stagnant water is the colour of faded amethyst, with a deserted boat by the shore. Why do I come here every morning? My fingers tingle in the cold grey mist, and I think how lovely it would be if we could walk here together, wading knee-deep in fallen leaves. But alone — how can the autumn breeze comfort me?

The delicate claws of time leave their traces on the silk. Here the ages passed like migrating birds, each leaving its mark, a scar left by fire. We let the endless scroll slip through our astonished fingers and then in the lowest corner write the modest characters of our own story.

The year has come and gone like a ribbon wound round a spool. I press my trembling hands to my breast to silence the alarm sounding there. I know you will come back. It may last for years, it may be in a few days, it may be in an hour. I shall lose myself in your embrace, casting off my burden of longing and sorrow. Hurry, hurry, life is short – spur your horse and ride up the path you know so well...

...I am waiting for you...

BIBLIOGRAPHY

Collection Pierre Barboutau: Peintures-estampes et objets d'art du Japon, I—II, 1904.

Albert Brockhaus: Netsuke, 1905.

O. Kümmel: Kunstgewerbe in Japan, 1911.

Catalogue of the First Portion of the Very Important Collection of Japanese Works of Art Formed by the Late Mr Walter Lionel Behrens of Manchester, 1913.

Maude Rex Allen: Japanese Art Motives, 1917.

V. F. Weber: Ko-ji ho-ten. Dictionnaire à l'usage des amateurs et collectionneurs d'objets d'art japonais et chinois, I—II, 1923.

M. J. Ballot: Les laques d'Extrême Orient, 1927.

O. Kümmel: Die Kunst Chinas, Japans und Koreas, 1929.

F. Meinertzhagen: The Art of the Netsuke Carver, London, 1955.

Vlasta Hilská: Histoire et Culture du peuple japonais, 1953.

Okada Yuzuru: Japanese Handicrafts, 1956.

E. Ryerson: The Netsuke of Japan, London, 1958.